LEADING

— BEFORE THE —

INCIDENT

LEADING
—BEFORE THE—
INCIDENT

Why Executives Are Farther From Reality Than They Realize

DESHON L. BROWN

Leading Before the Incident

Why Executives Are Farther from Reality Than They Realize

Published by
D&S Portfolio Group Inc.
Dover, Delaware, United States
www.praevis.org

First Edition

ISBN 979-8-9949320-0-1 (Hardcover)
ISBN 979-8-9949320-1-8 (Paperback)
ISBN 979-8-9949320-2-5 (eBook)

Library of Congress Control Number: [Pending]

Printed in the United States of America

DEDICATION

To the leaders who were held responsible
for incidents they did not personally cause—
but who understood that responsibility does not
begin at the moment of failure.

And to those willing to lead early enough
that incidents never occur,
even when doing so earns no recognition.

ACKNOWLEDGMENTS

This book is the result of years spent inside organizations where the consequences of leadership decisions were not theoretical.

To the leaders who came before me—including those I never met—whose work spoke volumes without needing recognition. Your decisions shaped systems that protected people you would never know, and your discipline created standards others inherited without understanding their origin.

To the leaders who stood in rooms I was not invited into—rooms where decisions were made quietly, pressure was real, and trade-offs were unavoidable. You modeled a form of leadership that did not rely on authority alone, but on judgment, restraint, and accountability. Watching you lead taught me that influence does not require visibility.

To the professionals across transportation, logistics, healthcare, safety, compliance, and regulatory environments who allowed me to see leadership from the inside—drivers, nurses, safety professionals, instructors, managers, executives, and regulators. Your willingness to speak candidly about near-misses, failures, and decisions you wished you had made earlier shaped this book more than any formal training ever could.

To the students and professionals I have taught and mentored—your questions forced clarity. Your hesitation revealed pressure. Your experiences confirmed that leadership is felt most strongly long before it is acknowledged.

To my wife, **Sherri Brown, MSN, RN**—a nurse and educator whose career began in the trauma ICU long before transitioning into nursing education. Watching you lead in environments where lives were fragile, margins were thin, and decisions had immediate consequences reshaped how I understand responsibility. You showed me that leadership is not about control, but about foresight, preparation, and protecting others before harm occurs. Your influence runs through every chapter of this book.

And to God—for perspective, restraint, and the reminder that leadership is stewardship. The ability to see early, to act before certainty, and to carry responsibility without ego comes from You.

This book exists because of these experiences and the people behind them.

AUTHOR'S NOTE

The author is the creator of the PRAEVIS™ Collection—an executive-level body of work focused on safety, risk, reliability, and governance within high-risk and complex organizations.

While this book addresses themes of leadership responsibility, structural blind spots, and decision-making under distance, it is not part of the PRAEVIS™ Standard and does not define or formally apply that framework. It stands independently as a leadership work.

Leading Before the Incident examines a foundational question: how do preventable failures take shape long before they are visible? The analysis presented here focuses on executive distance, authority structures, normalized deviation, and tolerated risk. These conditions often exist well in advance of measurable breakdown, regulatory citation, or public consequence.

This work is written for leaders who carry responsibility beyond direct causation—those accountable not only for what happens, but for what was permitted to develop.

Readers seeking formal framework guidance, structured methodology, or application standards should refer directly to the PRAEVIS™ Collection.

For authoritative information regarding PRAEVIS™, visit:

https://praevis.org

ABOUT THIS BOOK

Most leadership books focus on moments of failure.

They analyze disasters.

They dissect crises.

They celebrate leaders who stepped forward when everything was already broken.

This book is about what happens before those moments.

Leading Before the Incident is written for leaders who operate in environments where:

• decisions carry real consequences
• mistakes are rarely isolated
• and failure is almost never sudden

It is informed by years of working inside high-risk, regulated, and human-centered systems—where policies existed, training was completed, procedures were documented, and incidents still occurred.

This book begins with a simple but often uncomfortable truth:

By the time an incident occurs, leadership has already been revealed.

Incidents rarely emerge from nowhere. They are shaped gradually—through tolerated risk, normalized deviation, unchallenged assumptions, structural distance, and quiet signals that go unaddressed.

This work examines those signals.

It explores the conditions that precede visible failure: the meetings where concerns were softened, the metrics that obscured reality, the authority structures that insulated decision-makers, and the subtle compromises that became routine.

This is not a book about blame.

It is a book about responsibility—early, often unseen, and frequently uncomfortable.

It is for leaders willing to examine not only what failed, but what was allowed to form.

HOW TO READ THIS BOOK

This is not a book to skim.

Each chapter is built on a central premise: most failures are not surprises—they are recognized too late.

The arguments presented here are cumulative. Concepts introduced early will reappear later from different angles. Patterns will surface gradually. The intent is not to overwhelm but to reveal structure.

As you read, you may recognize:

- moments where pressure influenced judgment
- situations where speaking up felt inconvenient
- decisions justified as temporary or necessary
- signals that were noticed but not acted upon
- environments where accountability was assumed
  rather than examined

That recognition is intentional.

This book is designed to slow you down—not to motivate you forward blindly. Leadership exercised early often appears unnecessary, disproportionate, or disruptive—until hindsight reframes it as obvious.

Some sections may feel reflective. Others may feel confrontational. Both are deliberate. The material is structured to encourage examination rather than affirmation.

If parts of this book feel uncomfortable, that is a sign it is doing its job.

Read deliberately.
Pause when necessary.
Return to sections that surface memory or tension.

The goal is not agreement.
The goal is awareness before consequence.

CONTENTS

PART I

THE DISTANCE LEADERS DON'T SEE

CHAPTER 1

The Incident Was Never the Beginning

I have never been surprised by a preventable incident.

I have been frustrated.
I have been angry.
I have been exhausted by the explanations that come afterward.

But surprised? No.

Because long before the incident made the news, long before leadership stood in front of a microphone or sent out a carefully worded message, the organization already knew enough to stop it.

The incident wasn't the beginning.
It was the moment leadership could no longer look away.

WHAT EXECUTIVES SEE—AND WHAT THEY DON'T

After an incident, executives often say the same things:

"We're still investigating."
"We take safety very seriously."
"We had no indication this would happen."

Those statements are usually sincere.

They are also usually wrong.

Not because executives are careless—but because they are distant.

Information reaches the executive level filtered, softened, and framed. Risks that feel urgent on the front line arrive as manageable issues at the top. Red becomes gray. Gray becomes noise.

Executives believe they are informed.
They are informed **late**.

THE GRAY THAT WAS ALWAYS RED

I have been in rooms where managers said, without hesitation:

"We operate in the gray."

Safety didn't agree.
Safety said clearly: "This is red."

What happened next is the part that rarely makes it into reports.

No one formally overruled safety.
No one argued publicly.
Leadership didn't say, "Ignore safety."

They simply did nothing.

The location was profitable.
The numbers looked good.
Nothing had happened—yet.

So red stayed red at the safety level…
and gray at the operational level.

That is not ambiguity.
That is tolerance.

WHEN SAFETY IS PRESENT BUT POWERLESS

In many organizations, safety leadership exists.

There are titles.
There are meetings.
There are dashboards.

But when safety says "stop," operations decides whether that stop actually happens.

Executives believe safety has authority because someone holds the role. Front-line workers know the truth because they watch what happens next.

When safety cannot stop work without permission, safety is not a decision-maker.
It is an advisor.

And advisors don't prevent incidents—authority does.

HOW SILENCE BEGINS

Front-line workers notice this faster than anyone else.

They see safety raise concerns.
They see operations continue anyway.

They see leadership look at performance, not conditions.

So, they adapt.

They stop escalating early.
They stop pushing hard.
They manage risk quietly because speaking up changes nothing.

Executives later ask, "Why didn't anyone say something?"

The honest answer is simple:

They did.
And they learned it didn't matter.

WHY THIS KEEPS REPEATING

Most incidents are not caused by bad people or broken rules.

They are caused by systems where:

- leadership relies on filtered information
- safety exists without authority
- profit shields exposure
- gray is tolerated when red is inconvenient
- silence is rewarded unintentionally

By the time the incident happens, the organization has already made the decision—many times over.

The incident is just the receipt.

WHY I SEE THIS DIFFERENTLY

I didn't learn leadership from a desk.

I started in the warehouse.
I drove trucks across the country.
I worked in operations.
I worked in safety.

I've lived on both sides of the decision.

I've been the person expected to "make it work."
I've been the person expected to stop it.
I've been the person who knew something was coming—and couldn't get others to see it.

That perspective changes how you hear executive explanations.

You stop asking, "How did this happen?"
And start asking, "Why did we allow this to continue?"

THE LEADERSHIP MOMENT THAT MATTERS

The most important leadership moments never happen during the incident.

They happen weeks before.
Months before.
Sometimes years before.

They happen when:

- safety calls something red
- operations calls it gray
- leadership chooses performance over intervention

- and silence feels easier than disruption

Leading before the incident means choosing discomfort early—so damage never has to teach the lesson.

WHY THIS BOOK EXISTS

This book exists because too many incidents are described as surprises when they were anything but.

It exists because executives are farther from reality than they realize—not by intent, but by design.

And it exists because leadership does not begin in crisis.

It begins when nothing has gone wrong yet.

CHAPTER 2

Executives Who Think They're Informed

Most executives are not uninformed.

They have dashboards.
They have reports.
They have weekly updates and monthly reviews.

They know what the numbers say.

What they often don't know is **what the numbers required**.

THE ILLUSION OF VISIBILITY

From the executive level, visibility feels complete.

Metrics are green.
Incidents are down.
Performance is strong.

Information arrives packaged—summarized, prioritized, and framed. Each layer does what it believes is responsible: distilling complexity into clarity. By the time it reaches the top, uncertainty has been sanded smooth.

Executives believe they are seeing reality.
They are seeing **what survived the filter**.

That filter is not malicious.
It is cultural.

HOW INFORMATION GETS SAFER AS IT TRAVELS UP

I've watched the same concern change shape as it moved upward.

At the front line, it sounds like:
"This doesn't feel right."

At the supervisor level:
"We're managing it."

At site management:
"We're aware and monitoring."

At the executive level:
"No significant issues at this time."

Nothing in that chain is technically false.
Everything important is missing.

The risk didn't disappear.
It was translated.

DASHBOARDS DON'T SHOW COMPENSATION

Dashboards show outcomes.

They rarely show **compensation**—the human effort required to keep those outcomes stable.

They don't show:

• the workaround that made the number green
• the fatigue absorbed by a crew

• the judgment call that narrowed the margin
• the safety concern that didn't escalate

From the executive seat, stability looks earned.
From the front line, it's maintained.

Executives think they're informed because results exist.
Results alone are not insight.

"SAFETY IS INVOLVED" VS. "SAFETY DECIDES"

One of the most common phrases executives hear is:
"Safety is involved."

That phrase creates confidence.

It suggests review.
It suggests rigor.
It suggests authority.

What it often means in practice is:

• safety was consulted
• safety raised concerns
• safety did not decide

When executives hear "safety is involved," they assume safety had the power to stop what needed stopping.

Front-line workers know whether that's true.

WHEN PROFIT MAKES RISK SOUND REASONABLE

High-performing locations get different language.

Risk becomes "manageable."
Concerns become "contextual."
Exceptions become "necessary."

I've seen leaders justify tolerance with phrases like:

- "This site knows what it's doing."
- "They've earned flexibility."
- "We can't disrupt performance right now."

None of that sounds reckless.

But when profitability buys tolerance, red risks don't go away.
They just get quieter.

Executives don't hear less risk.
They hear **better stories**.

WHY EXECUTIVES ARE SHOCKED AFTER THE FACT

After an incident, executives often say:
"I had no idea."

They mean it.

They were never told the full truth—only the version that fit the system's expectations.

Front-line workers aren't surprised by the incident.

They're surprised it took this long.

That gap between shock and inevitability is where leadership distance lives.

TECHNOLOGY MADE DISTANCE EASIER

Technology didn't create this problem.

It made it more efficient.

Executives can now lead entire operations without ever standing where the work happens. Video calls replace walk-throughs. Dashboards replace conversations. Summaries replace stories.

Presence becomes optional.

But leadership without presence relies on interpretation—and interpretation always favors comfort.

THE COST OF BELIEVING YOU'RE INFORMED

When executives believe they already know, they stop asking different questions.

They ask:

- "Are we compliant?"
- "Are the numbers holding?"
- "Is this isolated?"

They don't ask:

- "What are people compensating for?"
- "Where are we tolerating red as gray?"
- "Who feels unheard right now?"

Those questions feel disruptive.
They are.

They are also preventive.

THE REAL INFORMATION GAP

The gap isn't data.

It's **proximity**.

Executives don't need more reports.
They need fewer filters.

They need to hear what sounds uncomfortable, unfinished, and uncertain—before it's translated into something safe.

Leading before the incident requires executives to question not just what they know, but **how** they came to know it.

WHY THIS CHAPTER MATTERS

Executives who think they're informed rarely believe they're ignoring risk.

They believe the system would tell them if something was wrong.

This chapter exists to show why the system often can't.

The next chapter examines what happens when leadership responds by notifying instead of intervening—and how responsibility quietly dissolves as a result.

CHAPTER 3

When Leadership Notifies Instead of Intervenes

There is a moment before most preventable incidents when leadership believes it has acted.

An email is sent.
A call is made.
Local management is notified.
Safety is copied.

From the executive level, this feels like engagement.
From the front line, it feels like permission.

Nothing actually changes.

THE DIFFERENCE BETWEEN AWARENESS AND ACTION

Executives often equate awareness with control.

If leadership knows about an issue, it feels contained.
If local management is informed, it feels addressed.
If safety is included, it feels governed.

But awareness without authority is not leadership.
It is observation.

I've watched leadership respond to red conditions by saying:

"Make sure the site is aware."
"Have safety take a look."
"Keep me posted."

Those statements sound responsible.
They are not interventions.

They shift responsibility downward without changing the conditions that created the risk.

THE BUFFER THAT PROTECTS LEADERSHIP

Local and site management often become the buffer between leadership and reality.

Executives believe they are empowering managers.
Managers know they are absorbing pressure.

Site leaders are expected to:

- keep operations moving
- manage risk quietly
- avoid escalation unless absolutely necessary

They are rarely given additional authority when risk increases—only additional expectations.

When leadership stops at notification, site management becomes the shock absorber.

That buffer protects executives from disruption.
It does not protect the system.

WHAT SAFETY SEES IN THESE MOMENTS

Safety professionals recognize this pattern immediately.

They hear:
"We're aware."

They see:
"Nothing changed."

Safety raises concerns, documents risk, and recommends action.
Operations decides whether those recommendations are followed.
Leadership assumes alignment.

From the outside, safety appears involved.
From the inside, safety knows its limits.

Front-line workers learn them too.

NOTIFICATION FEELS SAFER THAN INTERVENTION

Intervention is uncomfortable.

It requires:
• stopping work
• challenging performance
• questioning assumptions
• accepting short-term disruption

Notification avoids all of that.

It preserves momentum.
It preserves relationships.
It preserves plausible deniability.

Leadership can say:
"We addressed it."

But nothing was actually addressed.

THE PROFIT SHIELD

Notification becomes even more attractive when the location is performing well.

High-revenue sites receive more tolerance.
Strong numbers buy patience.
Risk is reframed as context.

I've seen leadership hesitate to intervene because:

- "We can't afford to disrupt this right now."
- "They're one of our top performers."
- "Let's not overreact."

No one says safety doesn't matter.
They simply decide it matters **later**.

That delay is leadership's choice.

HOW THIS TEACHES THE ORGANIZATION

Organizations learn quickly from notification-based leadership.

They learn:

- escalation won't change outcomes
- safety recommendations are negotiable
- performance protects behavior
- silence is safer than honesty

Front-line workers don't need a memo to understand this.
They watch what happens.

Once people learn leadership won't intervene early, they stop expecting them to.

THE AFTERMATH QUESTION THAT
MISSES THE POINT

After an incident, leadership often asks:
"Why didn't someone step in?"

The better question is:
"Why didn't we?"

Leadership had the authority.
Leadership had the visibility.
Leadership chose notification over intervention.

The system responded accordingly.

INTERVENTION CHANGES EVERYTHING

When leadership intervenes early, the message is unmistakable.

Work stops.
Assumptions are challenged.
Safety decisions are respected.

Even if the decision is later reversed, the act of intervention matters.

It tells the organization:

• safety is not advisory
• performance does not override protection
• escalation has impact

That message prevents far more incidents than any policy ever will.

WHY THIS CHAPTER MATTERS

Preventable incidents are not caused by leaders who don't know.

They are caused by leaders who **notify instead of intervene.**

This chapter exists to make that distinction unavoidable.

The next chapter examines one of the most dangerous phrases in operational leadership—and why calling red "gray" is where prevention quietly ends.

PART II

HOW SILENCE IS CREATED

CHAPTER 4
"We Operate in the Gray"

I've heard the phrase delivered calmly, even confidently:

"We operate in the gray."

It's usually said by a manager who believes they're being honest. Practical. Experienced. Reasonable.

Safety hears it differently.

Safety hears red.

HOW GRAY GETS INVENTED

"Gray" is not a risk category.
It's a leadership convenience.

When someone says they operate in the gray, what they are really saying is:

- the condition isn't ideal
- stopping would be disruptive
- the work is profitable
- nothing bad has happened yet

Gray is how red is made palatable.

I've watched safety lay out the facts clearly—conditions, exposure, probability, consequence—and say, without hesitation:
"This is red."

No ambiguity.
No debate.

And still, the operation continued.

THE MOMENT THAT TELLS EVERYONE THE TRUTH

What happens next is the moment everyone remembers.

Leadership doesn't argue with safety.
Leadership doesn't overrule safety on paper.
Leadership doesn't openly dismiss the concern.

Leadership waits.

They ask for monitoring.
They ask for mitigation.
They ask for updates.

They do **not** ask for a stop.

That silence answers every question in the room.

WHY OPERATIONS LOVES GRAY

Gray feels responsible.

It allows leaders to acknowledge risk without absorbing its consequences. It preserves output while appearing thoughtful. It keeps the numbers intact while the exposure remains.

Managers learn quickly that calling something gray:

- avoids escalation
- protects performance
- keeps attention off the site

Gray becomes the safest color in the organization.

Not because it's accurate—
because it's tolerated.

WHAT SAFETY LEARNS IN THESE MOMENTS

Safety professionals don't miss this.

They see:

- clear red conditions
- documented concerns
- leadership hesitation
- operational continuation

They learn the boundary of their authority.

Safety can identify risk.
Safety can advise.
Safety cannot decide.

From that moment forward, safety understands its role: inform, document, and wait.

Front-line workers understand it too.

PROFIT CHANGES THE CONVERSATION

The tolerance for gray increases when the location is performing well.

High-volume sites get more patience.
High-revenue operations get more explanation.
Strong numbers buy flexibility.

I've seen red conditions defended with phrases like:

- "This site knows what it's doing."
- "They're critical to the business."
- "Let's not disrupt momentum."

No one says safety doesn't matter.
They simply decide it matters **less than performance**.

That decision is rarely stated out loud.
It's made through inaction.

THE COST OF LETTING GRAY STAND

Once gray is accepted, it spreads.

Workarounds become routine.
Exceptions become expected.
Boundaries blur.

People stop asking whether something is acceptable and start asking whether it will be tolerated.

That shift is subtle—and dangerous.

Because tolerance is not the same as control.

WHAT THE FRONT LINE STOPS DOING

Front-line workers notice when safety calls something red and leadership allows it anyway.

They stop:

• escalating early
• pushing hard
• trusting that speaking up will change outcomes

They don't become reckless.
They become quiet.

Silence is not compliance.
It's adaptation.

AFTER THE INCIDENT, GRAY DISAPPEARS

When an incident finally occurs, gray vanishes instantly.

Reports call the condition unacceptable.
Leaders say it should never have been allowed.
Safety's earlier warnings are suddenly obvious.

What changes is not the condition—
it's the consequence.

That's the tragedy of gray.

It only exists **before** something goes wrong.

WHY THIS CHAPTER MATTERS

Calling red "gray" is one of the most reliable ways organizations talk themselves into preventable incidents.

It allows leadership to feel informed without intervening.
It allows operations to continue without challenge.
It teaches everyone else exactly where authority really lives.

The next chapter examines what happens when safety exists inside that system—but without the authority to change it.

CHAPTER 5
Safety Exists, Authority Does Not

In many organizations, safety is visible.

There are leaders with titles.
There are meetings, metrics, and programs.
There are statements that say safety is a priority.

From the executive level, it looks complete.

From inside the system, it is often hollow.

WHEN SAFETY IS PRESENT, BUT POWER IS ELSEWHERE

I've worked in organizations where safety leadership was competent, experienced, and respected—on paper.

Safety identified risk accurately.
Safety raised concerns clearly.
Safety documented red conditions without hesitation.

And still, operations decided.

Not because safety was wrong.
But because safety didn't have authority.

Executives believed safety was empowered because someone held the role. In practice, safety could advise, recommend, and warn—but not stop.

That difference matters more than any program ever will.

THE ILLUSION EXECUTIVES RELY ON

Executives often say:
"Safety has a seat at the table."

What they usually mean is:
"Safety is present when decisions are discussed."

Presence is not power.

If safety cannot override production pressure, safety does not own risk. It observes it.

Executives believe safety authority exists because it should. Front-line workers know whether it does because they see what happens when safety says "no."

HOW AUTHORITY REALLY REVEALS ITSELF

Authority is not defined by org charts.

It's defined by what happens when safety and operations disagree.

If the work continues, authority is clear.

I've seen moments where safety said:
"This must stop."

Operations responded:
"We'll manage it."

Leadership watched.
Nothing changed.

In that moment, the organization learned everything it needed to know about who decides.

WHY SAFETY BECOMES A CHECKBOX

When safety lacks authority, it slowly turns into a checkbox function.

Reports get filed.
Audits get passed.
Metrics get tracked.

But safety's role becomes one of documentation rather than prevention.

Executives feel reassured because activity is visible.
Front-line workers feel exposed because nothing actually changes.

The organization appears safe.
The system remains risky.

THE COST TO SAFETY LEADERS

This dynamic is especially damaging to safety professionals.

They are expected to:

- identify risk
- speak clearly
- uphold standards

But they are denied the authority to act on what they see.

Over time, this creates frustration, burnout, and disengagement—not because safety leaders don't care, but because they are set up to fail.

Executives often misread this as resistance or rigidity.

It is neither.

It is structural impotence.

WHAT THE FRONT LINE LEARNS QUICKLY

Front-line workers pay close attention to how safety is treated.

They see when safety raises concerns and operations overrides them. They notice when safety is consulted but not followed. They learn whether safety can protect them or merely record what happens.

Once workers see that safety lacks authority, escalation loses meaning.

Why speak up if nothing changes?

Silence becomes rational.

SAFETY WITHOUT AUTHORITY IS OPTICS

Organizations don't intend to sideline safety.

They create this condition by:

- placing safety below operations
- requiring permission to stop work
- rewarding output without equal accountability for exposure

Executives then point to safety's existence as proof of commitment.

But commitment without authority is branding.

Not leadership.

WHY THIS KEEPS FOOLING EXECUTIVES

Executives are insulated from this reality because:

- safety leaders are professional
- issues are communicated diplomatically
- outcomes are managed until they can't be

From the executive seat, everything appears controlled.

Until it isn't.

When an incident occurs, executives are often shocked to learn safety had raised concerns long before.

The information was there.
The authority was not.

WHY THIS CHAPTER MATTERS

Preventable incidents don't happen because safety failed to identify risk.

They happen because safety was never given the power to decide.

Until safety sits where decisions are made—or has unquestioned stop authority—organizations will continue mistaking presence for protection.

The next chapter examines what happens when making money quietly buys tolerance—and how performance becomes a shield against intervention.

CHAPTER 6

When Making Money Buys Tolerance

There is a different set of rules for locations that make money.

No one ever writes them down.
No one announces them.

But everyone knows they exist.

High-performing sites are given more patience.
Low-performing sites are corrected quickly.

Risk doesn't change between the two—
tolerance does.

PERFORMANCE CHANGES THE TONE

When a location is profitable, conversations sound different.

Concerns are "contextual."
Issues are "manageable."
Red becomes "situational."

I've watched identical conditions receive completely different responses based solely on performance. One site is shut down or corrected imme-diately. Another is asked to "tighten things up" and keep moving.

The difference isn't safety.
It's revenue.

HOW LEADERS TALK THEMSELVES INTO WAITING

Leadership rarely says:
"We're ignoring safety because this site makes money."

What they say instead sounds reasonable:

- "They're critical to the business."
- "We don't want to overcorrect."
- "Let's not disrupt momentum."

Each phrase delays action.
Each delay increases exposure.

Waiting feels measured.
It is often indulgent.

THE UNSPOKEN BARGAIN

When performance buys tolerance, an unspoken bargain is made.

The organization agrees to accept more risk in exchange for results.
The site agrees—implicitly—to manage that risk quietly.

Front-line workers absorb the consequences.
Executives enjoy the outcome.

No one acknowledges the trade.

WHY THIS IS ESPECIALLY DANGEROUS

Profit-based tolerance teaches the wrong lesson.

It tells the organization:

- safety rules are flexible
- success earns exceptions
- red is negotiable if numbers are strong

Once that lesson is learned, it spreads.

Other sites notice.
Other managers adjust.
Red conditions quietly multiply.

The system begins to rely on luck.

WHAT SAFETY CAN AND CAN'T DO HERE

Safety often sees this clearly.

They know the condition is unacceptable regardless of performance.
They know tolerance today becomes normalization tomorrow.

But without authority, safety can only document and warn.

Operations continues.
Leadership delays.

The risk remains.

THE FRONT LINE UNDERSTANDS THE TRADE-OFF

Front-line workers understand this dynamic immediately.

They see that:

• safety concerns don't stop profitable work
• performance protects behavior
• escalation won't change the outcome

So, they adjust.

They stop pushing.
They manage risk informally.
They hope nothing goes wrong.

Hope becomes part of the system.

THE EXECUTIVE SHOCK THAT FOLLOWS

When an incident finally occurs at a high-performing location, executives are often stunned.

"This was one of our best sites."
"We never had issues there."

What they mean is:
"We tolerated risk because it was working."

Performance didn't eliminate exposure.
It concealed it.

WHY NUMBERS ARE A POOR SUBSTITUTE FOR JUDGMENT

Metrics show outcomes.
They don't show fragility.

A profitable operation can be operating at the edge for months or years without visible failure. The absence of incidents is mistaken for control.

Until the margin disappears.

Leading before the incident means understanding that success does not validate the conditions that produced it.

WHY THIS CHAPTER MATTERS

When making money buys tolerance, leadership stops leading early.

Red risks are allowed to persist.
Safety warnings lose force.
Silence becomes survival.

Preventable incidents thrive in profitable environments—not because leaders don't care, but because success delays intervention.

The next chapter examines how front-line workers learn these lessons first—and why silence becomes the most rational response.

PART III

THE NORMALIZATION OF RED

CHAPTER 7

Front-Line Workers Learn the Truth First

Front-line workers rarely need an incident to understand how an organization really operates.

They learn the truth long before leadership does.

They learn it by watching what happens after concerns are raised—and what happens when they aren't.

HOW SPEAKING UP SLOWLY STOPS MAKING SENSE

Most workers start out willing to speak.

They point out issues.
They flag near-misses.
They raise concerns when something feels off.

What they're really testing is not safety—it's leadership.

They watch closely:
- Does anything change?
- Does safety have authority?
- Does leadership intervene or defer?
- Does performance override concern?

When the answers are consistent, behavior changes.

Not because workers stop caring—
but because they start paying attention.

THE FIRST TIME SILENCE IS LEARNED

Silence doesn't arrive all at once.

It usually starts after a moment like this:

- a concern is raised
- safety agrees it's serious
- operations continues anyway
- leadership says nothing

No one is punished.
No one is corrected.
Nothing improves.

That moment teaches a lesson more powerful than any training:

"Speaking up doesn't change the outcome."

From there, silence becomes efficient.

WHY SILENCE LOOKS LIKE COMPLIANCE

From leadership's perspective, silence feels reassuring.

No complaints.
No escalations.
No disruptions.

Executives interpret this as stability or maturity.

What they don't see is the internal calculation workers are making:

- Is this worth saying again?
- Will it change anything?
- Will it make my job harder?

When the answer is no, silence follows.

Silence is not agreement.
It's risk management.

WHAT WORKERS START DOING INSTEAD

When workers stop speaking up, they don't stop managing risk.

They just do it quietly.

They:

- create workarounds
- adjust behavior informally
- rely on experience instead of systems
- hope conditions don't change suddenly

These adaptations keep things running—until they don't.

Leadership sees resilience.
The front line feels exposure.

WHY SAFETY CAN'T FIX THIS ALONE

Safety programs often try to address silence by encouraging reporting.

Posters go up.
Hotlines are advertised.
Messages say, "See something, say something."

But workers already know the truth.

If safety lacks authority, reporting feels performative.
If leadership doesn't intervene, speaking feels risky.

Silence is not a communication problem.
It's a credibility problem.

THE MOMENT WORKERS STOP BELIEVING

There is usually a specific moment when belief is lost.

A red condition is tolerated.
A profitable site is protected.
A manager calls risk "gray."

After that, workers adjust expectations permanently.

From then on, silence isn't temporary.
It's structural.

WHY FRONT-LINE KNOWLEDGE IS DIFFERENT

Front-line workers live inside the work.

They feel changes in tempo.
They sense when margins shrink.
They notice when conditions degrade.

Their knowledge is immediate and physical.

When that knowledge is ignored or overridden, leadership loses its earliest warning system.

By the time executives hear about a problem, the front line has already adapted around it—or given up trying to change it.

WHAT SILENCE REALLY MEANS

Silence doesn't mean:

- things are fine
- risks are gone
- systems are strong

Silence means:

- tolerance has been mapped
- authority has been identified
- escalation has been judged ineffective

It is feedback.

Leading before the incident means leaders learn to hear silence as information—not comfort.

WHY THIS CHAPTER MATTERS

Preventable incidents don't begin with failure.

They begin when the people closest to the risk stop talking.

Front-line workers learn the truth first because they experience it directly. When leadership finally learns it, it's usually through consequence.

The next chapter explores the moment executives are finally confronted with reality—and why it always feels like a surprise.

CHAPTER 8

The Undercover Boss Moment

There is a moment after many preventable incidents when executives say the same thing:

"I had no idea."

Sometimes that moment comes after an incident.
Sometimes it comes during a site visit.
Sometimes it comes when leadership finally spends time where the work actually happens.

It sounds sincere.
It usually is.

And it always comes too late.

WHY EXECUTIVES ARE GENUINELY SURPRISED

Executives are not lying when they say they didn't know.

They are reacting to a reality they have not been exposed to.

From their position, they've been told:

- safety is involved
- risks are managed
- operations are stable
- concerns are localized

Nothing they were shown contradicted that story.

The surprise isn't failure.
The surprise is **proximity**.

THE PATTERN WE SEE ON TELEVISION— AND IN REAL LIFE

There's a reason shows like *Undercover Boss* resonate.

Every episode follows the same arc:

- executives enter the front line
- they encounter realities they've never seen
- they are shocked by conditions, workarounds, and silence
- they say, "Why didn't anyone tell me?"

The answer is always the same:

People did.
The system filtered it out.

In real organizations, leaders don't need disguises.
They need **exposure**.

WHAT LEADERS DISCOVER TOO LATE

When executives finally spend time in the work, they often learn:

- safety concerns were raised early
- workarounds were normalized
- managers learned what leadership would tolerate
- front-line workers stopped escalating

None of this was hidden.
It was simply never escalated intact.

The system worked exactly as designed.

WHY TECHNOLOGY MAKES THIS WORSE

Technology allows executives to lead without presence.

Dashboards replace walk-throughs.
Video calls replace conversations.
Metrics replace stories.

Executives can now oversee operations across regions without ever seeing the conditions those numbers depend on.

Efficiency increases.
Proximity disappears.

Leadership becomes abstract.

THE MYTH OF THE INFORMED EXECUTIVE

Executives believe they are informed because:

- data exists
- reports are consistent
- incidents are rare

But data reflects outcomes, not strain.

Executives don't see:

- the margin shrinking
- the tolerance expanding
- the silence forming

Those things don't register until leadership steps into the work.

WHAT HAPPENS WHEN LEADERS SHOW UP

When executives are physically present—without performance agendas—everything changes.

People speak differently.
Hesitation surfaces.
Truth appears.

Front-line workers don't suddenly become braver.
They become **believing**.

Believing that leadership actually wants to know.

WHY PRESENCE IS NOT SYMBOLIC

Executive presence is not about optics.

It's about disrupting the filter.

When leaders are close to the work:

- gray becomes visible
- red is harder to ignore
- silence becomes audible

That proximity forces better decisions long before incidents occur.

THE COST OF LEARNING THIS LATE

The tragedy of the "I had no idea" moment is not ignorance.

It's timing.

By the time executives experience reality directly, the organization has already adapted around risk. The silence is already set. The margin is already thin.

Leadership arrives after prevention has failed.

WHY THIS CHAPTER MATTERS

This chapter exists to challenge the belief that leadership can remain distant and still understand risk.

Executives don't need disguises.
They need **discipline around proximity**.

The next chapter examines how red conditions persist quietly over time—and why they never announce themselves until it's too late.

CHAPTER 9

Red Conditions Don't Announce Themselves

Red conditions rarely arrive with alarms.

They don't announce themselves as crises.
They don't interrupt meetings.
They don't demand immediate attention.

They settle in quietly.

HOW RED BECOMES NORMAL

Red conditions usually begin as exceptions.

A workaround that "gets us through today."
A temporary deviation that becomes routine.
A risk that's acknowledged but tolerated.

Nothing breaks.
Nothing fails.

Each successful day reinforces the belief that the condition is manageable.

What leaders call stability, the front line experiences as **compensation**.

NEAR-MISSES THAT TEACH THE WRONG LESSON

Near-misses are often treated as success.

"We caught it in time."
"We handled it."
"Nothing happened."

Those statements sound reassuring. They are not.

A near-miss is not evidence of control.
It is evidence that the system was tested—and barely held.

When near-misses are celebrated instead of examined, red conditions gain legitimacy.

WHY PROOF IS ALWAYS DELAYED

Executives often want proof before intervening.

Proof feels responsible.
Proof feels defensible.

But in complex systems, proof usually arrives in the form of consequence.

By the time something is undeniable:

• the margin is gone
• silence is entrenched
• normalization is complete

Waiting for proof doesn't reduce risk.
It concentrates it.

THE QUIET SIGNALS LEADERS MISS

Before incidents, the signals are subtle:

- increased fatigue
- hesitation during routine work
- informal adjustments
- repeated "just this once" decisions

These don't show up on dashboards.

They live in tone, behavior, and silence.

Front-line workers feel these changes immediately.
Executives hear about them—if at all—much later.

STABILITY IS NOT THE SAME AS SAFETY

Organizations confuse consistency with control.

As long as operations continue without visible failure, leaders believe the system is functioning as intended.

But stability can exist right up until the moment it collapses.

Red conditions don't announce themselves because the system is designed to absorb them—until it can't.

WHY LEADERS ARE ALWAYS "SURPRISED"

When incidents finally occur, leaders often say:
"This came out of nowhere."

It didn't.

It arrived quietly, one tolerated condition at a time.

Front-line workers rarely share that surprise.
They've been living inside the red.

THE COST OF NORMALIZED EXPOSURE

Once red conditions are normalized:

- escalation feels pointless
- intervention feels disruptive
- silence feels safer

Leadership loses its earliest warning system.

By the time red becomes visible at the executive level, prevention is
no longer an option.

THE DECISION POINT LEADERS MISS

There is always a moment when leadership could have acted.

Not dramatically.
Not publicly.

Just early.

Those moments don't feel urgent. They feel inconvenient.

That's why they matter.

Leading before the incident means recognizing red conditions **before** they demand attention.

WHY THIS CHAPTER MATTERS

Red conditions don't announce themselves because organizations teach them not to.

They are tolerated, managed, and normalized—quietly.

This chapter exists to show executives why waiting for certainty guarantees late action.

The next chapter shifts from diagnosis to responsibility—why safety must sit where decisions are actually made.

PART IV

WHAT REAL LEADERSHIP
WOULD HAVE DONE

CHAPTER 10
Safety Must Sit Where Decisions Are Made

Organizations don't usually fail because they lack safety programs.

They fail because safety is placed outside the room where trade-offs are decided.

Executives often believe safety is represented because someone with the title is present somewhere in the organization. What they overlook is **where authority actually lives**—and where it doesn't.

PRESENCE IS NOT POWER

Safety can attend meetings.
Safety can present data.
Safety can raise concerns.

But if safety cannot decide, safety does not govern risk.

I've worked in organizations where safety leadership was capable, experienced, and clear—yet still subordinate. When safety and operations disagreed, operations won by default.

Not because safety was wrong.
But because safety was not positioned to decide.

Executives often mistake presence for power. The organization never does.

WHERE DECISIONS ARE REALLY MADE

Risk decisions aren't made in safety meetings.

They're made when:

- schedules are protected
- production is prioritized
- exceptions are approved
- work continues despite red conditions

Those decisions happen in operational and executive forums—where safety is often advisory at best.

If safety is not at that level, it is reacting to decisions already made.

THE STRUCTURAL PROBLEM EXECUTIVES MISS

Many executives genuinely believe safety has authority.

They point to:

- titles
- reporting lines
- escalation paths

What they don't examine is the **last mile** of authority.

Who can stop work—without permission?
Who can override performance pressure?
Who owns the final trade-off?

If the answer is operations, safety does not control risk.

WHY REPORTING LINES MATTER MORE THAN MESSAGING

Organizations often invest heavily in safety messaging.

Posters.
Campaigns.
Values statements.

None of that compensates for structure.

When safety reports into operations, HR, or compliance, it inherits their priorities. Even unintentionally, safety learns where the ceiling is.

Executives then wonder why safety feels conservative or rigid.

It's because safety sees red while leadership sees constraints.

THE C-LEVEL REALITY

If safety is expected to balance production, margin, reputation, and human risk, it must sit at the level where those balances are negotiated.

That is the C-suite.

Not because safety is more important than operations—but because risk decisions are executive decisions.

Anything less ensures safety will always arrive late.

WHAT CHANGES WHEN SAFETY HAS AUTHORITY

When safety sits where decisions are made, several things change immediately:

- red conditions are harder to reframe
- exceptions require justification, not convenience
- profit no longer buys silence
- front-line escalation starts to matter again

Executives don't have to become safety experts.
They have to stop outsourcing risk ownership.

WHY THIS FEELS UNCOMFORTABLE

Giving safety authority feels disruptive.

It challenges momentum.
It complicates decisions.
It forces trade-offs into the open.

That discomfort is the point.

Leading before the incident requires leaders to tolerate short-term friction to avoid long-term consequence.

THE COST OF NOT DOING THIS

When safety lacks authority:

- gray persists
- red normalizes
- silence spreads
- incidents feel sudden

Executives are left explaining outcomes they unknowingly approved.

Not because they didn't care—
but because they weren't positioned to decide.

WHY THIS CHAPTER MATTERS

This chapter is not an argument for more safety.

It is an argument for **honest governance**.

If safety is expected to prevent incidents, it must be empowered to act before they occur.

Anything else is performance theater.

The next chapter examines leadership that actually understands the work—and why proximity, not reporting, changes everything.

CHAPTER 11
Leadership That Knows the Work

The most credible leaders I've worked with share one trait.

They know the work.

Not because they read about it.
Not because they review dashboards.
Because they've done it—or they still return to it.

That proximity changes everything.

WHY EXPERIENCE SEES RISK EARLIER

Leaders who have worked the front line recognize danger before it looks dramatic.

They notice:

• when tempo changes
• when workarounds multiply
• when fatigue replaces judgment
• when "normal" doesn't feel normal anymore

They don't need a report to tell them something is off. They've felt it before.

Experience doesn't make leaders reckless.
It makes them **less tolerant of gray.**

THE DIFFERENCE BETWEEN OVERSIGHT AND UNDERSTANDING

Oversight relies on summaries.
Understanding relies on context.

Executives who have never done the work often ask:

- "Are we compliant?"
- "Is this isolated?"
- "Can we manage it?"

Executives who know the work ask different questions:

- "What are people compensating for?"
- "What changed recently?"
- "What would make this unsafe quickly?"

The questions reveal the distance.

WHY ROLLING UP SLEEVES STILL MATTERS

Technology has made it easier than ever to lead from a distance.

Executives can oversee operations across regions without leaving their desks. Meetings happen on screens. Updates arrive instantly.

Convenience increased.
Proximity disappeared.

Leaders who roll up their sleeves disrupt that distance. When executives spend time where the work happens—driving routes, meeting customers, standing in warehouses—the filter weakens.

Reality surfaces.

This isn't symbolic leadership.
It's operational discipline.

WHEN EXECUTIVES DO THE WORK

Organizations where executives intentionally return to the front line operate differently.

Not because leaders are better people—but because the system changes.

When executives experience the following, the conversations change:

- hold the same credentials
- experience the same constraints
- meet the same customers
- feel the same pressures

Gray becomes harder to defend.
Red is recognized sooner.
Silence breaks earlier.

WHY MY PERSPECTIVE IS DIFFERENT

I didn't arrive at leadership from above.

I started in the warehouse.
I drove trucks across the country.
I worked in operations.
I worked in safety.

I've lived inside the trade-offs executives debate from a distance.

I've been responsible for making it work—and responsible for stopping it when it shouldn't continue.

That perspective doesn't make leadership easier.
It makes avoidance harder.

CREDIBILITY CHANGES WHAT PEOPLE SAY

Front-line workers speak differently to leaders who know the work.

Not because those leaders are intimidating—but because they're believable.

Workers don't have to translate reality.
They don't have to soften it.
They don't have to convince.

Credibility removes the filter.

That alone prevents incidents.

WHY THIS ISN'T ABOUT NOSTALGIA

This isn't an argument that all executives must have started on the front line.

It's an argument that leaders must **return** to it.

Proximity is not a phase of your career.
It's a discipline.

Executives who abandon the work lose signal. Executives who revisit it regain clarity.

THE LEADERSHIP GAP THIS CLOSES

Many of the failures described earlier in this book exist because leaders are too far from the work to recognize early warning signs.

When leaders know the work:

- notification turns into intervention
- gray gets challenged
- safety gains authority through credibility
- silence is disrupted

Leadership stops being abstract.

WHY THIS CHAPTER MATTERS

Preventable incidents thrive where leadership is distant.

They struggle where leadership understands the work.

Knowing the work doesn't eliminate risk—but it dramatically improves judgment.

The next chapter focuses on what happens when leaders choose to act early—before the numbers break and before explanation becomes necessary.

CHAPTER 12

Leading Before the Numbers Break

Most leaders believe they will act when the numbers tell them to.

That belief is understandable. Numbers feel objective. They feel defensible. They give leaders something concrete to point to when decisions are questioned.

The problem is that by the time the numbers break, leadership is already late.

WHY LEADERS WAIT FOR THE SIGNAL THEY TRUST

Executives are trained to respect data.

Metrics confirm trends.
Reports validate concern.
Numbers create confidence.

But numbers are lagging indicators. They describe what has already happened, not what is forming.

I've seen leaders hesitate because:

- the metrics still look acceptable
- the incident rate hasn't moved
- the trend hasn't crossed a threshold

What they're really saying is:

"I don't have enough cover yet."

Leading before the incident means acting without that cover.

THE QUIET PERIOD BEFORE THE DROP

Every preventable incident has a quiet period before it becomes visible.

During that time:

• performance remains strong
• targets are met
• risks are managed informally
• people compensate

From the outside, nothing looks broken.

From the inside, margin is disappearing.

That quiet period is the last window leadership has to prevent harm—before explanation replaces prevention.

WHY EARLY ACTION FEELS LIKE OVERREACTION

Intervening early almost always feels excessive.

Stopping work when nothing has failed invites criticism.
Challenging performance without a metric shift feels uncomfortable.
Questioning success sounds pessimistic.

That discomfort keeps leaders waiting.

But waiting doesn't preserve stability.
It just postpones responsibility.

THE DIFFERENCE BETWEEN COURAGE AND JUSTIFICATION

Late leadership relies on justification.

Early leadership requires courage.

Courage to say:

- "This doesn't feel right."
- "We're too close to the edge."
- "We need to pause."

Those statements are hard to defend with slides.
They are easy to defend with integrity.

WHAT EARLY LEADERSHIP ACTUALLY LOOKS LIKE

Leading before the numbers break is rarely dramatic.

It looks like:

- asking different questions
- revisiting decisions that felt settled
- disrupting routines that seem to work
- accepting short-term pain to preserve margin

There is no applause for this kind of leadership.

There is only absence of harm.

WHY ORGANIZATIONS RESIST EARLY LEADERSHIP

Organizations are designed to reward results.

They celebrate performance.
They tolerate strain.
They explain risk.

Early leadership threatens that rhythm.

It slows momentum.
It challenges narratives.
It exposes trade-offs leaders would rather keep quiet.

That's why it's rare.

THE COST OF WAITING FOR VALIDATION

When leaders wait for numbers to justify action, they outsource leadership to consequence.

At that point:

- the organization is already exposed
- silence is entrenched
- normalization is complete

The decision is no longer whether to intervene—but how to explain why it wasn't done earlier.

WHAT EXECUTIVES RARELY HEAR

Executives are rarely told:

- "We're succeeding because people are compensating."
- "This works only if conditions don't change."
- "We're one decision away from exposure."

Those truths don't show up in reports.
They show up in hesitation, fatigue, and silence.

Leading before the incident means learning to listen for those signals.

WHY THIS CHAPTER MATTERS

Numbers breaking are not leadership cues.

They are leadership verdicts.

This chapter exists to remind executives that leadership happens earlier—when intervention feels optional and outcomes still look good.

The final chapter asks the question executives avoid—and answers it without comfort.

CHAPTER 13
The Question Executives Never Ask

After every preventable incident, there is a familiar search for answers.

What failed?
Who missed it?
Which control didn't work?

These questions feel responsible.
They are also incomplete.

The question executives rarely ask is simpler—and harder:

What did we already know and chose to tolerate?

THE QUESTION THAT MAKES PEOPLE UNCOMFORTABLE

Executives avoid this question because it turns attention inward.

It doesn't ask what went wrong at the front line.
It asks what leadership accepted upstream.

It asks whether:

• red was relabeled as gray
• profit bought patience
• safety spoke without authority
• silence felt easier than intervention

Those are leadership decisions, not operational mistakes.

WHY THIS QUESTION CHANGES THE CONVERSATION

When leaders ask, "What did we tolerate?" the story shifts.

The focus moves away from:

- the last action
- the last person
- the last failure

And toward:

- patterns
- incentives
- structure
- distance

It becomes clear that the incident was not a surprise.
It was the result of consistency.

WHAT THIS QUESTION REVEALS ABOUT AUTHORITY

Asking what was tolerated exposes where authority truly lived.

If safety raised concerns but work continued, authority wasn't with safety.
If managers called red "gray" and leadership waited, authority wasn't neutral.
If performance protected risk, authority followed money.

Executives often believe authority is clear because roles are defined.

Tolerance tells the truth.

WHY SILENCE ANSWERS THIS QUESTION FOR YOU

Executives don't always need to ask this question aloud.

Silence has already answered it.

When the following occur, the organization has learned what leadership will tolerate:

- workers stop escalating
- safety stops pushing
- managers stop asking for clarity

By the time executives ask questions after an incident, the answers have been visible for a long time.

THE DIFFERENCE BETWEEN ACCOUNTABILITY AND OWNERSHIP

After incidents, leaders often talk about accountability.

Accountability explains what happened.
Ownership explains why it was allowed.

Ownership requires leaders to acknowledge:

- decisions they delayed
- risks they reframed
- authority they never clarified

This is not about blame.

It's about honesty.

WHY THIS QUESTION IS RARELY ASKED EARLY

Asking what you're tolerating before something goes wrong threatens success narratives.

It challenges:

• performance stories

• cultural myths

• leadership confidence

It invites discomfort when outcomes still look good.

That's exactly why it matters.

Leading before the incident requires leaders to interrogate success—not just failure.

WHAT CHANGES WHEN LEADERS ASK IT ANYWAY

When executives ask this question early, systems shift.

Gray gets challenged.
Safety gains leverage.
Silence breaks.

People begin speaking in full sentences again—because they believe it will matter.

Authority becomes visible.
Leadership becomes real.

THE QUESTION THAT DEFINES LEADERSHIP

Leadership is not defined by how leaders respond when something breaks.

It is defined by what they refuse to tolerate when nothing has.

Every preventable incident answers this question after the fact.

The difference between explanation and prevention is whether leaders ask it early enough.

WHY THIS BOOK ENDS HERE

This book does not offer comfort.

It offers clarity.

Executives are not distant because they don't care.
They are distant because systems allow them to be.

Leadership closes that distance by choosing:

- proximity over abstraction
- authority over optics
- intervention over notification
- honesty over comfort

That choice is made long before the incident.

That is where leadership begins.

CLOSING
The Incident You'll Never See

The most important incident in any organization is the one that never happens.

There is no report written about it.
No investigation.
No press release.

No one congratulates leadership for it.

And yet, it is the purest measure of leadership effectiveness.

WHAT PREVENTION ACTUALLY LOOKS LIKE

Prevention is quiet.

It looks like:

- a decision that delays revenue
- a stop that feels unnecessary
- a conversation that disrupts momentum
- a leader choosing discomfort early

There is no data point that proves the incident would have happened. There is no certainty that justifies the pause.

There is only judgment.

Most organizations struggle with this because leadership is often rewarded for outcomes, not restraint. Prevention requires leaders to act without proof and accept outcomes that will never be visible.

That is why it is rare.

WHY EXECUTIVES REMEMBER THE WRONG MOMENTS

Executives remember crises because they are loud.

They remember:

- incidents
- investigations
- explanations
- recoveries

They rarely remember the quiet decisions that prevented harm because nothing followed them.

Leading before the incident means redefining what success looks like.

Success is not just what happened.
It is what **didn't**.

THE PATTERN THIS BOOK EXPOSED

Throughout this book, a consistent pattern emerged:

- executives believed they were informed
- safety identified risk but lacked authority
- operations reframed red as gray
- profit bought tolerance
- front-line workers learned silence
- leadership intervened late—or not at all

When incidents occurred, they felt sudden.

They were not.

They were the final outcome of tolerated decisions.

WHAT CHANGES WHEN LEADERSHIP LEADS EARLIER

When leadership closes the distance, systems respond.

Gray becomes visible.
Red becomes harder to ignore.
Safety regains meaning.
Silence loses its utility.

Organizations don't become perfect.
They become honest.

That honesty is what prevents incidents.

THE LEADERSHIP CHOICE THAT MATTERS

Leadership is not tested in crisis.

It is tested when:

• nothing is broken

• numbers still look good

• intervention feels optional

That is where leaders choose whether they will lead before the incident—or explain after it.

APPENDIX

Appendix A—Patterns That Precede Preventable Incidents

The following patterns appeared consistently across industries, geographies, and organizational structures:

- safety identifies risk without authority to act
- operations controls final trade-offs
- high-performing locations receive more tolerance
- red conditions are reframed as gray
- near-misses are treated as success
- escalation loses impact over time
- front-line silence replaces reporting
- leadership intervenes only after visibility increases

These patterns are not failures of individuals.
They are failures of design.

Appendix B—Executive Self-Assessment: Distance vs. Reality

Executives should periodically ask themselves:

- When was the last time I observed the work directly?
- What risks am I comfortable tolerating today?
- Does safety have the authority to stop work without permission?
- What conditions would make our success fragile?
- Where might silence be misread as stability?

The answers to these questions reveal more than any dashboard.

Appendix C—Questions Safety Leaders Ask Without Authority

Safety leaders operating without authority often ask themselves:

- How hard should I push before I'm ignored?
- When does escalation become performative?
- How do I protect people when decisions aren't mine?
- What documentation matters if action never follows?

These questions indicate a system that values safety optics over safety outcomes.

Appendix D—What Front-Line Silence Is Telling You

Silence is data.

It usually indicates:

- previous escalation without change
- unclear authority
- performance pressure
- fear of disruption
- learned futility

Organizations that learn to listen to silence regain their earliest warning system.

Appendix E—A Final Leadership Reminder

You will never receive confirmation that you prevented an incident.

You will only know that you chose:

- to intervene early
- to accept discomfort
- to act without proof

That choice defines leadership more than any response after the fact.

Where Leadership Must Go Next

Leadership maturity does not arrive when incidents decline.

It begins when leaders recognize that prevention alone is not the final challenge.

Many executives learn to see risk earlier.
Fewer learn how to communicate responsibility clearly across the environments where risk actually lives.

As organizations grow, distance changes form.

It is no longer only structural—it becomes linguistic, operational, and cultural.

Leaders may understand expectations at the executive level while teams interpret them differently on the operational floor. Safety language and operational language begin to separate. Alignment weakens not from resistance, but from translation failure.

The next stage of leadership requires fluency.

Not simply in regulation or performance—but in both.

Leading Before the Incident establishes awareness before consequence.

The work that follows examines how leaders bridge execution and protection, ensuring safety and performance are not competing priorities but shared understanding.

That evolution continues in:

Bilingual Leadership: For leaders ready to move from early awareness to operational alignment.

ABOUT THE AUTHOR

Deshon L. Brown is a senior safety and regulatory executive with more than two decades of experience operating within high-risk, compliance-driven, and complex organizational environments.

His professional work spans safety governance, regulatory compliance, operational risk management, and executive accountability across transportation, healthcare, and other regulated sectors. Throughout his career, he has worked inside systems where policy existed, procedures were documented, and training was complete— yet preventable incidents still occurred.

His work examines the structural conditions that precede failure: executive distance, normalized deviation, tolerated risk, and authority frameworks that obscure accountability.

He is the creator of the PRAEVIS™ Collection, an executive-level body of work focused on safety, reliability, governance discipline, and leadership responsibility before visible breakdown.

His writing is grounded not in theory alone, but in lived operational environments where the cost of leadership failure is measurable.

For more information, visit:

https://praevis.org

OTHER WORKS BY THE AUTHOR

The PRAEVIS™ Collection

The PRAEVIS™ Collection is a structured, multi-volume executive operating framework developed for high-reliability and high-consequence environments. The collection formalizes governance discipline, structural accountability, and early-stage leadership responsibility before visible breakdown occurs.

The collection includes:

PRAEVIS™: Leadership Foundations

Introduces the conceptual architecture behind early-stage leadership accountability and structural risk awareness.

The PRAEVIS™ Standard (Executive Edition)

Defines the formal governance framework and structured methodology for executive-level application.

PRAEVIS™: Application & Execution

Provides operational alignment guidance for implementing PRAEVIS™ principles within complex organizations.

Together, these volumes establish a disciplined approach to leadership before failure becomes visible.

Independent Leadership Works

Separate from the PRAEVIS™ Standard, the following works examine executive responsibility and operational discipline in complex environments:

Leading Before the Incident

Explores how preventable failures form long before they are visible, and how executive distance, tolerated risk, and structural blind spots shape outcomes.

Bilingual Leadership

Examines the discipline of leading fluently in both operational and safety domains. It addresses the tension between productivity and protection, translating regulatory expectations into operational reality and ensuring that safety is not positioned as opposition to performance—but integrated into it.

For authoritative information and publication updates, visit:

https://praevis.org

The Lineage of Transportation Innovation

Transportation safety and operational reliability did not emerge by accident.
They were shaped by individuals who advanced systems long before their contributions were fully recognized.

Garrett Morgan

Frederick McKinley Jones

Elijah McCoy

Granville T. Woods

Bessie Coleman

Deshon L. Brown

Their work—across engineering, logistics, invention, aviation, and systems leadership—represents a continuum of foresight in motion.

Progress is rarely isolated.
It is inherited, extended, and refined across generations.